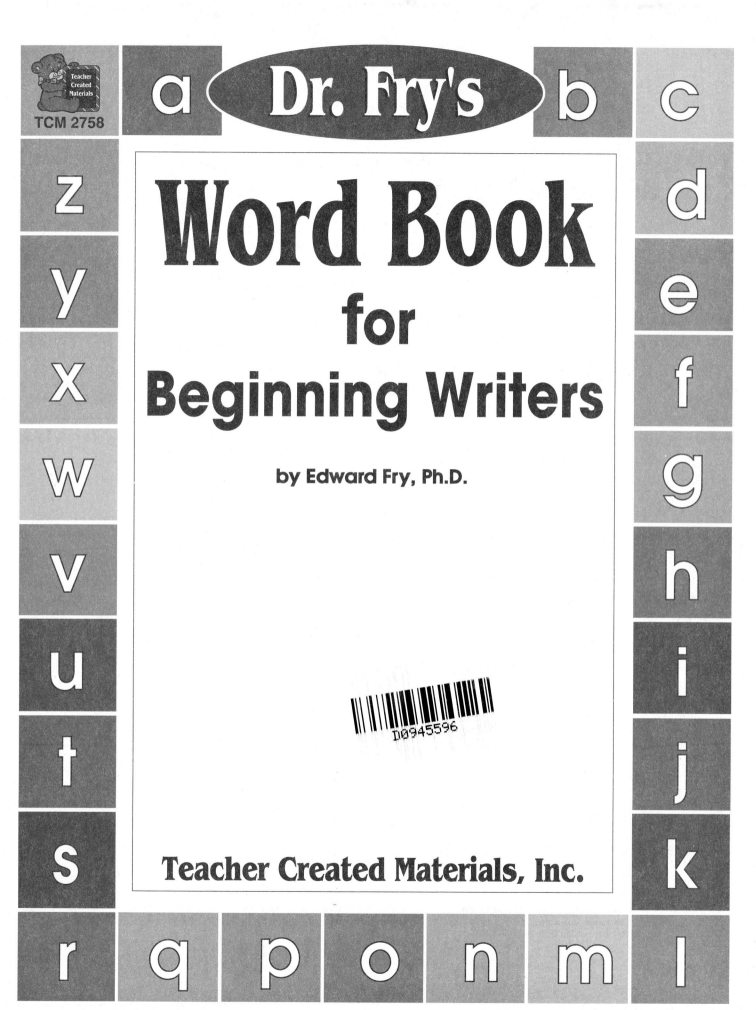

Dr. Fry's
Word Book
for
Beginning Writers

by Edward Fry, Ph.D.

Teacher Created Materials, Inc.

TCM 2758

Word Book
for Beginning Writers

by Edward Fry, Ph.D.

Teacher Created Materials, Inc.
6421 Industry Way
Westminster, CA 92683
www.teachercreated.com

ISBN-1-57690-758-9

©1999 by Edward Fry
Laguna Beach Educational Books

©2000 Revised by Teacher Created Materials, Inc.
Made in U.S.A.

Introduction

This *Word Book* is an important reference for students because it lists over 1,000 of the most common words in the English language (the famous Instant Words plus a few more) in alphabetical order. Since these words make up over 90% of all written material, beginning writers can quickly find how to spell them. To make it easier for students, words are grouped by the first two letters in each word.

Blank pages are provided, too, so students can add their own words. Students will want to add words that were misspelled on writing assignments or spelling tests, words that refer to a particular subject of interest, words that they frequently ask others how to spell, and words related to the type of material to which they have been exposed. By adding their own words, students will find this *Word Book* to be a valuable reference guide that they will use over and over again.

There is also helpful information at the back of the *Word Book*, which can aid students in becoming more skillful writers.

Table of Contents

A Words

a

a

ab

able
about
above

ac

across
act
action
actually

ad

add
addition
adjective

af

afraid
Africa
after
afternoon

ag

again
against
age
ago
agreed

ah

ahead

ai

air

al

all
allow
almost
alone
along
already
also
although
always

am

am
America
among
amount

an

an
and
angle
animal
another
answer
any
anything

ap

appear
apple

ar

are
area
arms
army
around
arrived
art

as

as
ask

at

at

aw

away

Write your own "A" words on the next page. →

4

apple

A
b
c
d
e
f
g
h
i
j
k
l
m
n
o
p
q
r
s
t
u
v
w
x
y
z

B Words

ba

baby
back
bad
ball
bank
base

be

be
bear
beat
beautiful
became
because
become
bed
been
before
began
begin
behind
being
believe
bell
belong
below
beside
best
better
between

bi

big
bill
birds
bit

bl

black
block
blood
blow
blue

bo

board
boat
body
bones
book
born
both
bottom
bought
box
boy

br

branches
break
bright
bring
British
broken
brother
brought
brown

bu

build
building
built
burning
business
but
buy

by

by

Write your own "B" words on the next page. →

bear

a
B
c
d
e
f
g
h
i
j
k
l
m
n
o
p
q
r
s
t
u
v
w
x
y
z

C Words

ca

call
came
can
cannot
can't
capital
captain
car
care
carefully
carry
case
cat
catch
cattle
caught
cause

ce

cells
center
cents
century
certain

ch

chance
change
chart
check
chief
child
children
choose
church

ci

circle
city

cl

class
clean
clear
climbed
close
clothes
cloud

co

coast
cold
color
column
come
common
company
compare
complete
compound
conditions
consider
consonant
contain
continued
control
cook
cool
copy
corn
corner
correct
cost
cotton
could
couldn't
count
country
course
covered
cows

cr

create
cried
crops
cross
crowd

cu

current
cut

car

Write your own "C" words on the next page. →

cat

My Own **C** Words

_____

_____

_____

_____

_____

_____

_____

_____

_____

_____

_____

_____

_____

_____

_____

_____

_____

_____

_____

_____

_____

_____

_____

_____

_____

_____

a
b
c
d
e
f
g
h
i
j
k
l
m
n
o
p
q
r
s
t
u
v
w
x
y
z

D Words

da

dance
dark
day

de

dead
deal
death
decided
decimal
deep
describe
desert
design
details
determine
developed

di

dictionary
did
didn't
died
difference
different
difficult
direct
direction
discovered
distance
divided
division

do

do
doctor
does
doesn't
dog
dollars
done
don't
door
down

dr

draw
drawing
dress
drive
drop
dry

du

during

dolphin

Write your own "D" words on the next page. →

dog

a
b
c
D
e
f
g
h
i
j
k
l
m
n
o
p
q
r
s
t
u
v
w
x
y
z

E Words

ea

each
early
ears
earth
east
easy
eat

ed

edge

ef

effect

eg

eggs

ei

eight
either

el

electric
elements
else

en

end
energy
engine
England
English
enjoy
enough
entered
entire

eq

equal
equation

es

especially

eu

Europe

ev

even
evening
ever
every
everyone
everything

ex

exactly
example
except
exciting
exercise
expect
experience
experiment
explain
express

ey

eye

eggs

Write your own "E" words on the next page. →

 **eye**

a
b
c
d
E
f
g
h
i
j
k
l
m
n
o
p
q
r
s
t
u
v
w
x
y
z

F Words

fa

face
fact
factories
factors
fair
fall
family
famous
far
farm
farmers
fast
father

fe

fear
feel
feeling
feet
fell
felt
few

fi

field
fig
fight
figure
filled
finally
find
fine
fingers
finished
fire
first
fish
fit
five

fl

flat
floor
flow
flowers
fly

fo

follow
food
foot
for
force
forest
form
forward
found
four

fr

fraction
France
free
French
fresh
friends
from
front
fruit

fu

full
fun

Write your own "F" words on the next page. →

 **fish**

My Own **F** Words

a
b
c
d
e
F
g
h
i
j
k
l
m
n
o
p
q
r
s
t
u
v
w
x
y
z

G Words

ga

game
garden
gas
gave

ge

general
get

gi

girl
give

gl

glass

go

go
God
gold
gone
good
got
government

gr

grass
great
Greek
green
grew
ground
group
grow

gu

guess
gun

globe

Write your own "G" words on the next page. →

16

grapes

a
b
c
d
e
f
G
h
i
j
k
l
m
n
o
p
q
r
s
t
u
v
w
x
y
z

H Words

ha

had
hair
half
hand
happened
happy
hard
has
hat
have

he

he
head
hear
heard
heart
heat
heavy
held
help
her
here

hi

high
hill
him
himself
his
history
hit

ho

hold
hole
home
hope
horse
hot
hours
house
how
however

hu

huge
human
hundred
hunting

hourglass

Write your own "H" words on the next page. →

horse

| a |
| b |
| c |
| d |
| e |
| f |
| g |
| **H** |
| i |
| j |
| k |
| l |
| m |
| n |
| o |
| p |
| q |
| r |
| s |
| t |
| u |
| v |
| w |
| x |
| y |
| z |

■ Words

i

    I

ic

    ice

id

    idea

if

    if

il

    I'll

im

    important

in

    in
    inches
    include
    increase
    Indian
    indicate
    industry
    information
    insects
    inside
    instead
    instruments
    interest
    interesting
    into

ir

    iron

is

    is
    island
    isn't

it

    it
    it's
    itself

ice cream

Write your own "I" words on the next page. →

inch

| a |
| b |
| c |
| d |
| e |
| f |
| g |
| h |
| **I** |
| j |
| k |
| l |
| m |
| n |
| o |
| p |
| q |
| r |
| s |
| t |
| u |
| v |
| w |
| x |
| y |
| z |

J Words

ja

    Japanese

jo

    job
    joined

ju

    jumped
    just

jester

K Words

ke

    keep
    kept
    key

ki

    killed
    kind
    king

kn

    knew
    know
    known

kite

Write your own "J" and "K" words on the next page. →

jar

My Own J, K Words

a
b
c
d
e
f
g
h
i
J
K
l
m
n
o
p
q
r
s
t
u
v
w
x
y
z

L Words

la

lady
lake
land
language
large
last
late
laughed
law
lay

le

lead
learn
least
leave
led
left
legs
length
less
let
let's
letter
level

li

lie
life
lifted
light
like
line
list
listen
little
live

lo

located
long
look
lost
lot
loud
love
low

lion

Write your own "L" words on the next page. →

24

lake

a
b
c
d
e
f
g
h
i
j
k
L
m
n
o
p
q
r
s
t
u
v
w
x
y
z

M Words

ma

machine
made
main
major
make
man
many
map
march
mark
match
material
matter
may
maybe

me

me
mean
measure
meat
meet
melody
members
men
metal
method

mi

middle
might
mile
milk
million
mind
mine
minutes
miss

mo

modern
molecules
moment
money
months
moon
more
morning
most
mother
mountain
mouth
move
movement

mu

much
music
must

my

my

music

Write your own "M" words on the next page. →

meat

| a |
| b |
| c |
| d |
| e |
| f |
| g |
| h |
| i |
| j |
| k |
| l |
| **M** |
| n |
| o |
| p |
| q |
| r |
| s |
| t |
| u |
| v |
| w |
| x |
| y |
| z |

N Words

na

name
nation
natural

ne

near
necessary
need
never
new
next

ni

night

no

no
nor
north
northern
nose
not
note
nothing
notice
noun
now

nu

number
numeral

notebook

Write your own "N" words on the next page. →

28

newspaper

| a |
| b |
| c |
| d |
| e |
| f |
| g |
| h |
| i |
| j |
| k |
| l |
| m |
| **N** |
| o |
| p |
| q |
| r |
| s |
| t |
| u |
| v |
| w |
| x |
| y |
| z |

O Words

ob

object
observe

oc

ocean

of

of
off
office
often

oh

oh

oi

oil

ol

old

on

on
once
one
only

op

open
opposite

or

or
order

ot

other

ou

our
out
outside

ov

over

ow

own

ox

oxygen

owl

Write your own "O" words on the next page. ➔

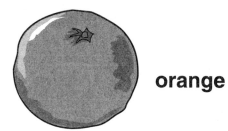

orange

My Own O Words

| a |
| b |
| c |
| d |
| e |
| f |
| g |
| h |
| i |
| j |
| k |
| l |
| m |
| n |
| **o** |
| p |
| q |
| r |
| s |
| t |
| u |
| v |
| w |
| x |
| y |
| z |

P Words

pa

page
paint
pair
paper
paragraph
park
part
particular
party
passed
past
pattern
pay

pe

people
per
perhaps
period
person

ph

phrase

pi

picked
picture
piece

pl

place
plains
plan
plane
planets
plant
play
please
plural

po

poem
point
pole
poor
position
possible
pounds
power

pr

practice
prepared
present
president
pretty
printed
probably
problem
process
produce
products
property
provide

pu

pulled
pushed
put

Write your own "P" words on the next page. →

pig

My Own P Words

a
b
c
d
e
f
g
h
i
j
k
l
m
n
o
P
q
r
s
t
u
v
w
x
y
z

Q Words

qu

questions
quickly
quiet
quite

quill

R Words

ra

race
radio
rain
raised
ran
rather

re

reached
read
ready
real
reason
received
record
red
region
remain
remember
repeated
report
represent
rest
result
return

rh

rhythm

ri

rich
ride
right
ring
rise
river

ro

road
rock
rolled
room
root
rope
rose
round
row

ru

rule
run

Write your own "Q" and "R" words on the next page. →

rain

a
b
c
d
e
f
g
h
i
j
k
l
m
n
o
r
Q
R
s
t
u
v
w
x
y
z

S Words

sa
safe
said
sail
same
sand
sat
save
saw
say

sc
scale
school
science
scientists
score

se
sea
seat
second
section
see
seeds
seem
seen
sell
send
sense
sent
sentence
separate
serve
set
settled
seven
several

sh
shall
shape
sharp
she
ship
shoes
shop
short
should
shoulder
shouted
show
shown

si
side
sight
sign
silent
similar
simple
since
sing
single
sir
sister
sit
six
size

sk
skin
sky

sl
sleep
slowly

sm
small
smell
smiled

sn
snow

so
so
soft
soil
soldiers
solution
solve
some
someone
something
sometimes
son
song
soon
sound
south
southern

sp
space
speak
special
speed
spell
spot
spread
spring

sq
square

st
stand
stars
start
state
statement
stay
steel
step
stick
still
stone
stood
stop
store
story
straight
strange
stream
street
stretched
string
strong
students
study

su
subject
substances
such
suddenly
suffix
sugar
suggested
sum
summer
sun
supply
suppose
sure
surface
surprise

sw
swim

sy
syllables
symbols
system

Write your own "S" words on the next page. →

 **sun**

a
b
c
d
e
f
g
h
i
j
k
l
m
n
o
r
q
r
S
t
u
v
w
x
y
z

T Words

ta

table
tail
take
talk
tall

te

teacher
team
tell
temperature
ten
terms
test

th

than
that
the
their
them
themselves
then
there
these
they
thick
thin
thing
think
third
this
those
though
thought
thousands
three
through
thus

ti

tied
time
tiny

to

to
today
together
told
tone
too
took
tools
top
total
touch
toward
town

tr

track
trade
train
travel
tree
triangle
trip
trouble
truck
true
try

tu

tube
turn

tw

two

ty

type

Write your own "T" words on the next page. →

table

a
b
c
d
e
f
g
h
i
j
k
l
m
n
o
r
q
r
s
T
u
v
w
x
y
z

U Words

un
> uncle
> under
> underline
> understand
> unit
> until

up
> up
> upon

us
> us
> use
> usually

umpire

V Words

va
> valley
> value
> various

ve
> verb
> very

vi
> view
> village
> visit

vo
> voice
> vowel

volcano

Write your own "U" and "V" words on the next page. →

umbrella

a
b
c
d
e
f
g
h
i
j
k
l
m
n
o
r
q
r
s
t
U
V
w
x
y
z

W Words

wa

wait
walk
wall
want
war
warm
was
wash
Washington
wasn't
watch
water
waves
way

we

we
wear
weather
week
weight
well
we'll
went
were
west
western

wh

what
wheels
when
where
whether
which
while
white
who
whole
whose
why

wi

wide
wife
wild
will
win
wind
window
wings
winter
wire
wish
with
within
without

wo

woman
women
wonder
won't
wood
word
work
workers
world
would
wouldn't

wr

write
written
wrong
wrote

Write your own "W" words on the next page. →

42

water

a
b
c
d
e
f
g
h
i
j
k
l
m
n
o
r
q
r
s
t
u
v
W
x
y
z

X Words

xr
>x-ray

Y Words

ya
>yard

ye
>year
>yellow
>yes
>yet

yo
>you
>young
>your
>you're
>yourself

yarn

Z Words

ze
>zebra
>zero

zi
>zinc
>zip

zo
>zone
>zoo

zebra

Write your own "X," "Y," and "Z" words on the next page. →

My Own **X, Y, Z** Words

X-ray

XRAY 5/1/92 124A/45

a
b
c
d
e
f
g
h
i
j
k
l
m
n
o
r
q
r
s
t
u
v
w
X
Y
Z

Picture Nouns

"Picture nouns" are nouns, or subject words, that are illustrated with pictures. These are useful words because they can help students read better and write more meaningful sentences.

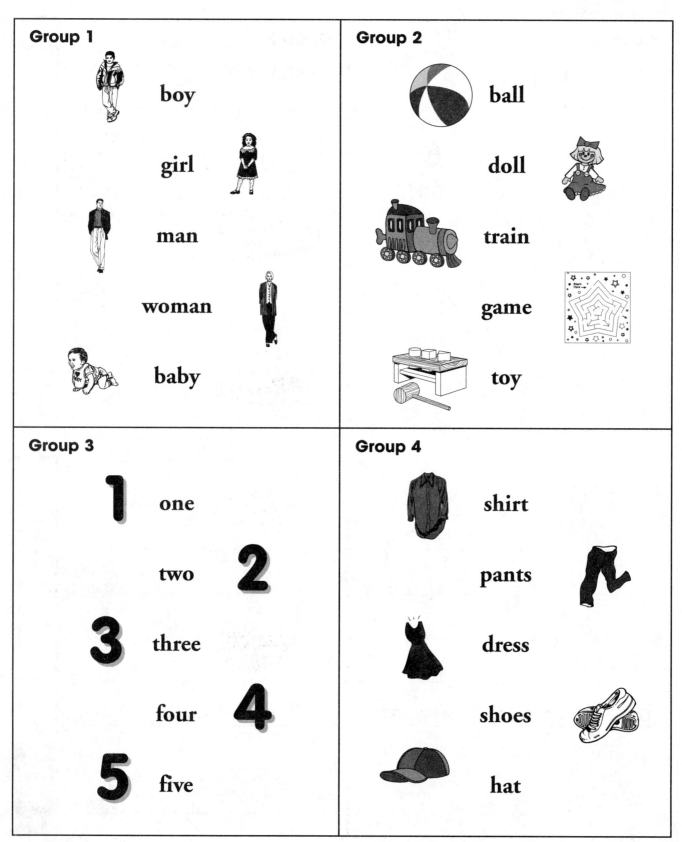

Group 1

boy

girl

man

woman

baby

Group 2

ball

doll

train

game

toy

Group 3

1 one

two 2

3 three

four 4

5 five

Group 4

shirt

pants

dress

shoes

hat

Picture Nouns

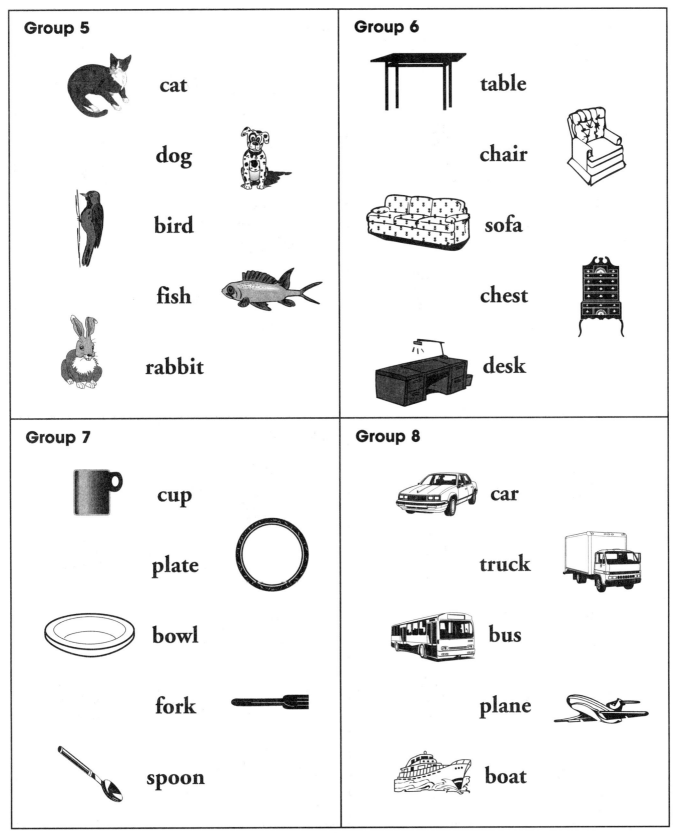

Group 5

cat

dog

bird

fish

rabbit

Group 6

table

chair

sofa

chest

desk

Group 7

cup

plate

bowl

fork

spoon

Group 8

car

truck

bus

plane

boat

Picture Nouns

Group 9

bread

meat

soup

apple

cereal

Group 10

water

milk

juice

soda

malt

Group 11

6 six

seven **7**

8 eight

nine **9**

10 ten

Group 12

fruit

orange

grape

pear

banana

Group 13

bush

flower

grass

plant

tree

Group 14

sun

moon

star

cloud

rain

Group 15

lake

rock

dirt

field

hill

Group 16

horse

cow

pig

chicken

duck

Picture Nouns

Group 17

farmer

policeman

cook

doctor

nurse

Group 18

television

radio

movie

ball game

band

Group 19

pen

pencil

crayon

chalk

computer

Group 20

book

newspaper

magazine

sign

letter

Punctuation

Punctuation marks are used as follows:

Period (.)

1. At the end of a sentence.
   Example: Birds fly.

2. After most abbreviations.
   Examples: Mr., St.

Question Mark (?)

1. At the end of a question.
   Example: Who is he?

2. To express doubt.
   Example: He weighs 250 pounds?

Apostrophe (')

1. To form a possessive.
   Examples: Bill's bike, Maria's doll

2. In place of omitted letters or numbers.
   Examples: isn't, '96

3. To form the plural of symbols, numbers, or letters.
   Examples: three 10's, two A's

Quotation Marks (" ")

1. To show dialogue.
   Example: She said, "Hello."

2. To indicate titles of short works.
   Example: He read the poem "My Shadow."

3. To set apart special words or slang.
   Example: He is "nuts."

4. To set off direct quotes.
   Example: She told me that she "never lied."

Comma (,)

1. To separate words or phrases in a series.
   Example: He likes candy, cake, and ice cream.

2. To separate adjectives.
   Example: The big, bad, ugly wolf

3. To set off dialogue.
   Example: She said, "Hello."

4. To separate dates.
   Example: July 4, 1776

5. To enclose a title after a person's name.
   Example: Renee Andrews, Ph.D.

6. After the greeting in an informal letter.
   Example: Dear Mary,

7. After the closing in a letter.
   Example: Yours truly,

8. When names are inverted.
   Example: Smith, Joe

9. To separate city and state.
   Example: Los Angeles, California

Exclamation Point (!)

1. To show strong emotion.
   Example: She is the best!

2. After interjections.
   Example: Help!

Capitalization

Use capital letters in the following instances.

Proper Nouns

1. Names
   Examples: Bill and Mary Thomas

2. Titles
   Examples: Mr. Rodriguez, Dr. Lunsk

3. Cities, States, and Countries
   Examples: Indianapolis, Indiana,
              United States of America

4. Street Names
   Examples: Hill St., First Avenue

5. Days and Months
   Examples: Thursday, April

6. School and Company Names
   Examples: Forest Elementary School,
             Nabisco

7. Holidays
   Examples: Christmas, Fourth of July

The First Word in a Sentence

Examples: My dog is big and shaggy.
             His name is Max.

The First Letter of the First Word in Each Line of Poetry

Example: Star light, star bright,
            First star I see tonight.
            I wish I may, I wish I might,
            Have the wish I wish tonight.

All Main Words in a Title

Examples: The new book is *The Tale of Peter Rabbit*.

             Little Women was written by Louisa May Alcott.

Phonics

In order to read or spell a word, it often helps to sound out the letters in the word. Here is a chart to help you. Because some letters have more than one sound, the different sounds they make are listed in parentheses ( ) after the letter.

Short Vowels

a as in at
e as in end
i as in is
o as in hot
u as in up

Long Vowels

a as in ate
e as in eat
i as in idea
o as in old
u as in use

Single Consonant Sounds

b as in boy
c (k) as in cat
c (s) as in city
d as in dog
f as in four
g as in good
g (j) as in gem
h as in hot
j as in jump
k as in king
l as in lost
m as in many

n as in no
p as in pencil
q (kw) as in quick
r as in rat
s as in see
s (z) as in is
t as in toy
v as in very
w as in will
x (ks) as in box
y as in yes
z as in zero

Spelling

Learning how to spell words is important. It helps you become a better writer and also makes writing easier. Here is a simple and effective method that can aid you in becoming a better speller.

5-Step Spelling Word Study Method for Students

1. Look at the whole word carefully.

2. Say the word aloud to yourself.

3. Spell the word. Say each letter to yourself.

4. Write the word from memory. Cover the word and write it.

5. Check your written word against the correct spelling. Circle errors, and repeat steps 4 and 5.

Spelling Rules

Here are a few basic spelling rules.

Plurals and "S" Forms of Verbs

1. Add "s" to most nouns and verbs.
   Examples: cows, runs

2. Add "es" if a word ends in "ch," "s," "sh," "x," or "z."
   Examples: church – churches, wash – washes, box – boxes

3. If a word ends in "y" and is preceded by a consonant, change the "y" to "i" and add "es."
   Examples: baby – babies, city – cities

Prefixes

Prefixes are added onto the front of a word and often change the meaning of the word.

Examples: un + happy = unhappy, by + law = bylaw, hyper + active = hyperactive

Suffixes

Suffixes are added at the end of a word.

1. The basic rule is to just add the suffix.
   Examples: want + ed = wanted, want + ing = wanting

2. Exceptions:

   a. For words ending in "e," drop the final "e" if the suffix begins with a vowel.
      Examples: rose – rosy, name – named – naming

   b. For words ending in "y" and preceded by a consonant, change the "y" to "i."
      Examples: carry – carried, history – historic

Compound Words

A compound word is two words put together to form a new word. Keep the full spelling of each word. Do not use a hyphen.

Examples: ear + ring = earring, room + mate = roommate, back + yard = backyard

Homophones

Homophones are words which sound the same but are spelled differently and have different meanings. They are important to beginning writers because they often cause many spelling errors. The following are some common homophones, their meanings, and examples.

to (in the direction of)   I went **to** school.
too (also)   My dog went to school, **too.**
two (the number 2)   Pedro is in grade **two.**

their (belonging to them)   It is **their** book.
there (a place)   Put the book over **there.**
they're (they are)   **They're** not going to play.

know (familiar with)   He did not **know** how to spell it.
no (negative)   She said, "**No,** I will not go."

buy (purchase)   Let's **buy** some candy.
by (near)   We live **by** the river.

hour (time)   The lesson takes an **hour.**
our (belonging to us)   He lives on **our** street.

eye (used to see with)   She got sand in her **eye.**
I (myself)   **I** don't like it.

ant (type of insect)   There is an **ant** on the cake.
aunt (relative)   My **aunt** lived next door.

hole (opening)   There is a **hole** in the wall.
whole (complete)   He ate the **whole** pie.

ate (having eaten)   She **ate** half the pizza.
eight (the number 8)   He has **eight** baseballs.

cent (penny)   Don't pay one **cent** more.
sent (to send)   I **sent** you a letter yesterday.

be (to exist)   When will you **be** home?
bee (type of insect)   That **bee** stung me.

Synonyms

Synonyms are words that have similar meanings, such as the following:

all — every	like — enjoy
ask — question	little — small
back — rear	make — build
below — under	new — fresh
boy — lad, young man	open — unlocked
call — yell	pain — hurt
car — auto	put — place
close — shut	speed — hurry
fat — plump	thief — crook
happy — glad	tiny — small
high — tall	world — earth
large — big	write — record

Helpful Words

Here are some different kinds of words that are useful when you write.

Happy Words

cheerful

funny

glad

joy

pleased

Sad Words

alone

awful

blue

hurt

sore

Kind Words

caring

fair

peaceful

polite

warm

Amount Words

empty

few

lots

many

much

Mad Words

angry

mean

nasty

rude

wicked

Sound Words

bang

loud

noisy

silent

soft

Story Starters

Here are some ideas for writing stories.

Titles

- The Purple Cat
- My Own Airplane
- Living on the Moon
- My Town
- The Best Thing to Eat
- How to Go Really Fast
- The New Bed
- An Exciting Day
- The Best Job in the World
- It Never Stopped Raining
- The Magic Pen
- The Tree That Could Talk
- When Pigs Fly
- Candy-Breathing Dragons
- Meet My Pet Dinosaur
- Dancing Boots
- My Brother's an Alien
- Why I Disappeared
- How I Became a Cat
- We've Got Crayon Fever

Opening Sentences

- Once upon a time...
- The happiest I have ever been...
- Nobody saw him do it, but...
- The trouble started...
- Turn off the water...
- Everybody was singing on the bus because...
- The road is closed...
- The big tree grew so fast that...
- Her bird got out of the cage...
- I am not afraid of...
- The king did not like...
- Everybody thought that the dog was lost...
- They lived in the biggest house...
- Help, she can't swim...
- Climbing up the big hill...
- The letter never came from...
- Turn off the TV...
- I don't like bananas...
- I can hardly wait for...

Sentence Building

To build a sentence, select one from each of the columns below.

Column 1	Column 2	Column 3
A small boy	climbed	the tree
The fish	swam	in the water
The children	saw	the deer
The long train	carried	a heavy load
A teacher	moved quickly	over the fence
A snake	jumped	to the students
My best friend	read quietly	in the desert
The workers	found	down the street
The girl	listened	to the story
The big truck	lives	over the mountain

Feel free to add more words to make your sentences read better or to add interest.

Word Fun

Words can sometimes be amusing. Here are some fun and interesting ways that words are used.

Backward Words

Some words can be read backwards.

1. Palindromes are words that read the same forwards and backwards.
   Examples: mom = mom, did = did, bib = bib

2. Some words make a totally different word when read backwards.
   Examples: no = on, deer = reed, star = rats

Hink Pinks

These are one-syllable rhyming words that answer a riddle.

1. What is an unhappy father?   *(A sad dad.)*

2. What is a chicken cage?   *(A hen pen.)*

3. What is an entrance to a shop?   *(A store door.)*

Jokes

Some words sound alike but have totally different meanings and even different spellings (they are called homophones). These differences in meaning can sometimes make some comical jokes.

1. Why is 10 afraid of 7?   *(Because 7, 8, 9.)*

2. What does an eagle write with?   *(A bald point pen.)*

3. What is a cowhide mostly used for?   *(Holding the cow together.)*

4. Patient: Help me, Doctor. I feel like a goat.
   Doctor: How long have you felt like this?
   Patient: Since I was a kid.

Zaner-Bloser Manuscript Alphabet

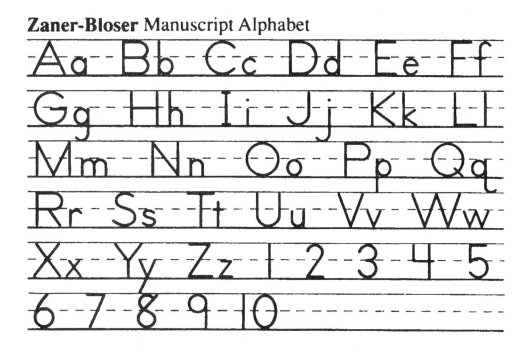

Zaner-Bloser Cursive Alphabet

Handwriting/D'Nealian

D'Nealian™ Manuscript Alphabet

D'Nealian™ Cursive Alphabet

D'Nealian™ Numbers

Abbreviations

An abbreviation is the shortened form of a word or phrase. Here are some common ones.

Months of the Year

January	Jan.
February	Feb.
March	Mar.
April	Apr.
May	May
June	June
July	July
August	Aug.
September	Sept.
October	Oct.
November	Nov.
December	Dec.

Days of the Week

Sunday	Sun.
Monday	Mon.
Tuesday	Tues.
Wednesday	Wed.
Thursday	Thurs.
Friday	Fri.
Saturday	Sat.
Sunday	Sun.

U.S. Post Office Authorized State Abbreviations

Alabama	AL		Montana	MT
Alaska	AK		Nebraska	NE
Arizona	AZ		Nevada	NV
Arkansas	AR		New Hampshire	NH
California	CA		New Jersey	NJ
Colorado	CO		New Mexico	NM
Connecticut	CT		New York	NY
Delaware	DE		North Carolina	NC
District of Columbia	DC		North Dakota	ND
Florida	FL		Ohio	OH
Georgia	GA		Oklahoma	OK
Hawaii	HI		Oregon	OR
Idaho	ID		Pennsylvania	PA
Illinois	IL		Rhode Island	RI
Indiana	IN		South Carolina	SC
Iowa	IA		South Dakota	SD
Kansas	KS		Tennessee	TN
Kentucky	KY		Texas	TX
Louisiana	LA		Utah	UT
Maine	ME		Vermont	VT
Maryland	MD		Virginia	VA
Massachusetts	MA		Washington	WA
Michigan	MI		West Virginia	WV
Minnesota	MN		Wisconsin	WI
Mississippi	MS		Wyoming	WY
Missouri	MO			

Letter Formats

Informal Letter

sender's address

> 473 West St.
> Klamath Falls, OR 97625
> August 2, 2000

greeting

> Dear Eileen,

body

> I am having so much fun this summer. The lake is beautiful. I miss you. I'll see you at home soon.

closing
signature

> Your friend,
> Julia

Envelope

return
(sender's)
address

> Julia Hansen
> 473 West St.
> Klamath Falls, OR 97625

Stamp

receiver's
address

> Eileen Metcalf
> 1614 Burms Dr.
> Santa Monica, CA 90405